HAMILTON
IMAGES OF A CITY

View of Hamilton from Sam Lawrence Park

HAMILTON
IMAGES OF A CITY

PHOTOGRAPHY AND TEXT BY

RICHARD KOSYDAR

PUBLISHED BY

TIERCERON PRESS

Published in Canada by: **Tierceron Press**
76 Maple Avenue
Dundas, Ontario L9H 4W4
Telephone: (905) 628-9092

Canadian Cataloguing in Publication Data

Kosydar, Richard
        Hamilton : images of a city

ISBN 0-9694077-3-4

    1. Hamilton (Ont.)--Pictorial works. I. Title.

FC3098.37.K68 1999   971.3'5204'0222   C99-900654-1
F1059.5.H2K68 l999

Film preparation by Eclipse Colour, Burlington, Ontario

Printed in Canada by Friesens

Front Cover: The rooftop plaza above Jackson Square
Back Cover: View of Hamilton and the Dundas Valley

Acknowledgments

I wish to thank Patricia Peacock-Evans, Hamilton artist-illustrator, for kind permission to reprint (on page 106) her lovely sketches of historic Dundas houses, which originally appeared in *Beyond Paradise: Building Dundas 1793-1950*.

Toronto Architect Alan Seymour provided and gave permission to use the beautiful commemorative lithograph (reproduced on page 7) of the original 140-year-old print of St. Paul's Presbyterian Church. Chromolithographs from the original print are available at a very reasonable price from: Canadian Historical Reproductions, 53 Turner Road, Toronto, Ontario M6G 3H7.

I am grateful to Mary Anderson, whose Ph.D. research for McMaster University's English Department is based upon the Whitehern archives, for bringing to my attention the important and under-appreciated role played by Thomas B. McQuesten in the evolution of Hamilton's landscape.

Walter Peace, Professor of Geography at McMaster University, provided numbers of helpful leads in obtaining historical material, as well as insightful observations.

Brian Henley, Head of Special Collections at the Hamilton Public Library, was extremely helpful in providing the great majority of original black-and-white historical photographs.

The City of Hamilton gave permission to use material from The *Hamilton* and *Scourge* Foundation's book, ***Ghost Ships (Hamilton & Scourge: Historical Treasures from the War of 1812)***, by Emily Cain (publ. 1983).

One of the delights of learning about Hamilton's history was the opportunity to attend a guided tour of the Hamilton Cemetery, led by volunteer historical interpreter Gary Hill. Mr. Hill offers engaging, informative tours of the Cemetery from April through September, revealing many fascinating details of the city's history.

Eclipse Colour provided high quality products, and it was a pleasure to work with their competent, congenial personnel.

My wife, Eleanore contributed the photograph of the rock-strewn base of Websters Falls (page 111); she assisted with the commentary, and edited the text. I greatly appreciate all of her help, and her unflagging cheerful encouragement and support.

McMaster University Engineering buildings are seen across the main square. As late as the 1920's, Hamilton was the only major city in Ontario not to have an institution of higher learning. At the same time McMaster was a small struggling Baptist university in downtown Toronto: a move to Hamilton would be good for both parties. The Baptists felt they could not accept help from the public purse, although they needed outside help to make the costly move. The citizens of Hamilton, ranging from children to corporations, responded over the summer of 1928 and raised a needed share of the funds. The city's Board of Parks Management was instrumental in ensuring that the University had the necessary land, with landscaped grounds, on favourable terms in Westdale, in part through the donation of a 50-acre parcel of land.

Foreword

This book was inspired by a passing comment Mary Anderson made to my wife Eleanore. It seems that Mary's friend Bev Everest had been looking for a nice colour coffee table book of Hamilton to give as a gift and could not find one. It occurred to me that this would make an excellent theme for my next book. I wish I were gentleman enough to say that this book was written only for Bev, but alas this is not the case. The niche market she identified was what I had been looking for.

Ten years ago my wife and I produced a coffee table book on the natural beauty of the Dundas area, which sold out in less than three years and for which there is still a demand. We then did a book on the Niagara Escarpment which is currently "in print" (that's a polite way of saying it hasn't sold out). Our costs on that book have been recovered, and it is now earning a profit. After an initial round of activity to get it established, the book seems to have settled in quite nicely as a tourist and gift item and is taking care of itself. It is sold all along the Escarpment from Niagara Falls to Tobermory.

The book I envisaged for Hamilton would bring out the beauty of the city and its environs, and be well-suited as the little memento that brings out fond feelings in us for our community. Most of the images are of familiar buildings or landscapes that people can recognise, but done with a little flair, or from a slightly different viewpoint.

This pictorial book presents images that I feel symbolise Hamilton. Other authors have captured its human history in words and pictures exceptionally well, whereas I have tried to capture on film a series of images that typify the actual city itself. These range from steel mills to downtown structures and streets, to McMaster University and the beauty of the city's parks and natural setting.

Recognising the strong interest people have in the history of their community, I felt that a number of historical images juxtaposed with the colour photos would add a welcome element and would illustrate how the Hamilton landscape has changed over time. Being a landscape photographer, I deliberately chose not to include people or cars in the photos. All photographs get converted into computer images as part of the printing process and hence it was easy to edit out any wayward objects such as human beings.

Hamilton is an inherently photogenic city. A number of features make it so: its topography, its steel industry and numerous very attractive buildings. There is the watery expanse of the Bay, and the bars that separate the bodies of water—the beach strip that sets Burlington Bay apart from Lake Ontario, and Burlington Heights which separates the Bay from Cootes Paradise. The Escarpment that surrounds the city adds a rugged interest.

I feel that the steel mills are, per square kilometre, the most photogenic features in Hamilton. And this from someone who spends, and has spent, a considerable amount of time wandering in the picturesque hills of the Dundas Valley well to the city's west. The massive forms of the steel mills combined with some good lighting make for strong compositions. My wife and I had to work hard to get the pictures for our books of natural landscapes. In contrast, taking the photographs of Hamilton for this book was easy—surprisingly so.

There are two sides to Hamilton: the east side and the west side. The east end is the home of industry and industrial air. The west side is the home of the hills and waters of the Dundas Valley; of McMaster University and air which is more breathable. By its nature the smelting and fabricating of iron and steel is a dirty business—though less so with new technologies. Office buildings and university campuses are clearly more genteel than blast furnaces. Steel mills and their fumes are what everyone who crosses the Skyway Bridges sees, and associates with the city. The west side receives little press. The arrangement of photographs in this book plays on this theme constantly, and seeks to give its due to Hamilton's other, less familiar side.

St. Paul's Presbyterian Church, on the corner of James and Jackson Streets, was completed in 1854. Designed by English architect William Thomas, it is an outstanding example of Canadian Victorian church architecture. Its 80-foot spire is mounted atop a 100-foot tower, and is the only spire in Ontario to be constructed of stone. Masonry towers are very susceptible to any earth movement, and while Hamilton is not known as a seismically active area, minor earth tremors do occur. In 1944 some damage, which was quickly repaired, resulted from a minor quake .

A coloured lithograph of St. Paul's was created at the time the church was built; it was restored and reproduced in a limited edition to commemorate a major restoration of the church in 1990. This coloured lithograph is a work of art and is available at a very reasonable price. (See Acknowledgments for further details.)

Maclure & Macdonald Lithrs. Glasgow 1855/
Canadian Historical Reproductions, Toronto 1990

Introduction

Hamilton is generally known as an industrial city: an iron and steel city, to be specific. Its mills and the industries connected with them have shaped the city and its character to a considerable degree. They are what most outsiders and indeed, most of its inhabitants associate with the city. Yet Hamilton has another distinguishing feature that is not as well-known, but is equally well-developed: its extensive system of parks and conservation areas. This book looks closely at both these aspects of the community.

Hemmed in by the Bay on the north and the Niagara Escarpment to the south, the city originally developed a long and narrow profile between these two prominent features. The "Mountain" was a formidable obstacle for early generations; and for about one hundred years, access up and down its face was severely restricted. With good roads and powerful means of propulsion we barely notice "Hamilton Mountain" today. But if we had to drag ourselves up it without these advantages, we would have a better appreciation of what earlier generations of Hamiltonians faced.

Only three significant roads climbed the Escarpment in the nineteenth century: the James Street access, the Jolley Cut and Beckett Drive. All were rough and difficult roads. It was not until the 1930's that the Sherman Cut and its east and west access roads were blasted out; and only in the 1950's and later were the major four-lane roads constructed.

Two inclined railways once scaled the Escarpment face. One was built at James Street in 1892, and one at Wentworth Street in 1899. Each had two sets of rails, and two cars that counterbalanced one other so that the engines pulled only the weight of the passengers and vehicles on board. Although the structures looked risky, in the forty years that the inclines were in business (during which millions of trips were made up and down) there do not seem to have been any serious accidents. Farm and commercial wagons were the major users of the inclines, but family outings to the top of the brow for the view and air were also common. Like the old electric radial lines, they fell victim to the automobile in the 1930's.

Manufacturing came easily to Hamilton. From its earliest days in the 1830's as a town on the edge of the western agricultural frontier in Ontario, foundrymen, mostly from the United States, came and established factories to produce agricultural implements and other goods such as stoves that were of value to the settlers. At this time, the interior of southwestern Ontario was still a wilderness just being opened up.

With the coming of the railroad in the mid-1850's, small factories were joined by much larger enterprises—the railroad shops. The foundations for a manufacturing city were being put in place. Hamilton's first railroad, the Great Western Railroad, set up shops along the southwest corner of the bay. Here locomotives were assembled and serviced. A rolling mill was built to reroll English rails so they could withstand the colder Canadian winters. Over the next thirty years a wide variety of metalworking factories producing goods ranging from nails to bridge girders were established in the area. Iron and steel fabricating became second nature to this community.

The introduction of import tariffs by the Macdonald government led to more investment in Canada by American companies seeking to avoid the tariffs. The Hamilton Blast Furnace Company was founded and produced its first iron in 1895. It was amalgamated with a number of other metalworking companies to form the Steel Company of Canada. Another example of industrial migration was the International Harvester Company, a manufacturer of agricultural equipment which came to the city in 1903. Hamilton by then was well on the way to becoming an industrial city.

Commerce did not come so easily. The town was originally founded as a trading centre at the head of navigation on Lake Ontario and the edge of the agricultural frontier. With the coming of the Great Western Railway in 1855, many Hamiltonians hoped that their city would become the predominant commercial capital of the country. Local entrepreneurs had hoped the railways would create a commercial empire based on sinews of steel rails.

That honour was to go instead to Toronto, which had a number of strategic advantages. The major provincial east-west route from Montreal to Windsor goes through Toronto, but misses Hamilton—note how even now, Highway 401 passes north of the latter. Toronto was also the natural terminus for the Trans-Canada railway line from the West. And it not only possessed its own sheltered harbour; it was the legislative capital of the province and would gain the perks that flowed from that position.

On the other side of Lake Ontario, the shortest route between Detroit and Buffalo lies to the south of Hamilton. In short, the most important routes bypass the city; and Hamilton's regional dominance has been confined to a limited area to its west and south.

If Hamilton's hopes for becoming a major commercial and business centre did not materialise, the city was nevertheless destined to become a major industrial centre. Its protected harbour on the Great Lakes with ample undeveloped waterfront properties, good railway connections, central location vis-à-vis the major markets, and a smart and aggressive business class stood it in good stead when conditions were ripe for major industrial growth at the turn of the last century.

The other notable aspect of Hamilton is its unusually beautiful natural endowment. At the heart of this endowment are Burlington Bay and the "Mountain." Hamilton is a valley city with a good-sized body of water near its centre. It

Cootes Paradise

is located within the Dundas Valley, which has been cut deeply into the Niagara Escarpment by the action of rivers and glaciers. The Escarpment's steep face made it unsuitable for building. Large tracts of this rugged topography are publicly owned and are accessible to the public for recreational use. The Bay, which made the harbour and the steel industries possible, also provided the city with wetlands such as Cootes Paradise that have been set aside as nature preserves.

Only in the 20th century has the city's natural heritage been appreciated to any extent. During two major periods of the city's

history, park lands and open spaces were set aside in significant amounts. In the 1920's and 1930's, the Hamilton Board of Parks Management under the leadership of Thomas B. McQuesten and Cecil V. Langs purchased land falling more or less within the city boundaries. Later in the century, during the 1960's and 1970's, the Hamilton Region Conservation Authority acquired large acreages of ruggedly beautiful hills and valleys within the Dundas Valley. Currently there is a major push underway to not only clean up and restore the ecological integrity of the Bay, but to make its western part attractive and accessible for public enjoyment.

Viewed as a whole, Hamilton reveals itself to be a truly diverse and well-rounded urban centre. In addition to its strong industrial base, balanced by a rich natural heritage, the city possesses many fine examples of architectural and artistic achievement, academic and cultural excellence, and historical interest. Furthermore, it was designated in 1993 as a Model Community by the International Council for Local Environmental Initiatives, in recognition of the restoration of Hamilton harbour and of broad-ranging regional "Vision 2020" initiatives.

Rather than perpetuate the limited vision of Hamilton as a steel city, I prefer to see it as a "well-forged"city. Through the efforts of an unusually talented and ambitious group of individuals over the course of a century and a half, Hamilton has been shaped from its natural setting and inherent advantages into the robust, versatile, attractive city we see today.

Hamilton Central School, completed in 1853, is the oldest school in Hamilton. It was built for 1,000 students and was in its time the largest graded school in the province. In 1891 it underwent a major renovation that changed it from "a squat and gloomy old castellated edifice" into "a stately pile, with lofty tower." The roof slope was steepened and the central tower made taller. The apartment buildings on either side of the school were built in the 1960's and 1970's.

The Hamilton Club, located at James and Main in a rather quiet brown brick house, was for many years an exclusive club for Hamilton's social elite. It is also a place where the business and professional elite can socialise and talk business. The club has been at its present location since it became a legal entity in 1873. The present house dates back to 1908, when it replaced another structure on the same site. Originally a men's club, women were first admitted in 1960. Today it is not as exclusive as it was earlier in this century, and many successful business and professional people now belong who would not be considered part of the "upper crust."

The unusually well-executed Beaux Arts structure across the road to its left was designed as a bank at the turn of the century. It has been tastefully renovated and is now a commercial office building.

Hess Village, near the core of the city, is a four-block area around Hess and George Streets. During the 1970's, its attractive but old and somewhat rundown single and semi-detached Victorian houses were converted into shops, restaurants and offices. A lawyer began the process with the renovation of a structure for his law office, and then continued with other buildings. Care was taken to maintain the Victorian character of the structures.

Within Hess Village, a block of George Street between Bay and Hess was closed off to vehicular traffic and covered with concrete pavers, making for an attractive pedestrian way. This block is noted more for night life than it is for early morning activity (which is when this photograph was taken).

Hess Street and Village take their name from the Hess family, who were among the original settlers to the region and owned hundreds of acres when it was still farmland in the early 1800's.

The handsome Irving Zucker Sculpture Court, adjacent to the Art Gallery of Hamilton and Hamilton Place, features several striking bronze sculptures by distinguished artists. Shown here are two views of "The Source," by Sorel Etrog, with the Art Gallery and the Sheraton Hotel (above) and the Convention Centre and Hamilton Place (right) in the background.

The rooftop garden plaza above downtown Hamilton's Jackson Square is adjacent to the Central Branch of Hamilton Public Library (located just left of the camera). It offers a partial view of City Hall, now almost 40 years old, seen beyond the Sheraton Hotel (the brick building to the right). The plaza is an oasis of calm and beauty in the centre of the city.

The Legacy of Thomas Baker McQuesten

One individual in particular, Thomas B. McQuesten, exerted an unusually profound influence on the development of the Hamilton landscape.

The McQuesten family history spanned three generations in Hamilton. In 1839, Dr. Calvin McQuesten left the United States for Canada, giving up a successful career in medicine to align his fortunes with the city at the head of Lake Ontario and the edge of the agricultural frontier. Along with other entrepreneurs, he perceived an opportunity here for industrial development. He established an iron foundry which imported iron from England or America to fabricate into goods such as stoves and agricultural implements. A skilled businessman, he was able to amass a considerable personal fortune over the next 20 years.

The family fortune was subsequently lost by Calvin's son and heir, Isaac, whose business acumen did not match that of his father. Isaac invested the family fortune in manufacturing ventures that failed. Alcoholism and depression were also recurring problems in his short life. He married the capable Mary Baker, a minister's daughter who was to contribute to the social fabric of the city in her own right, and who bore him seven children. Their sixth was Thomas Baker McQuesten, a mere six years old at the time of his father's death but destined to alter the face of Hamilton.

Mary raised her young brood alone in the large family home named "Whitehern" (which is Scottish for "White House"). An aristocrat by birth and breeding, she had been left with this large house, a high social standing which she took seriously, and very little income. She devoted her considerable energy to rearing her children, to church and social work, and to maintaining her home and its grounds to be a place of beauty. It was here that Tom at an early age absorbed his mother's love of gardening. He and his siblings also absorbed her strict upbringing, and grew into a close-knit family dominated totally and utterly by their formidable mother.

Great hopes were pinned upon Tom, who attended the University of Toronto to study political science and then law, receiving his law degree in 1907. His mother saw him as the principal source of income for this impoverished family of high social standing, and she was not about to lose him to a potential wife. It is

A plaque commemorating T. B. McQuesten's contributions is located just north of the High Level Bridge.

likely that Mary Baker McQuesten adhered to a prevailing belief in eugenics, which may have fortified her in opposing her children's marital prospects—certainly none had the fortitude to contradict her opposition, and may have agreed that family tendencies to alcoholism and mental instability ought not to be passed on to future generations.

Thomas McQuesten was to devote his life with almost missionary zeal to politics and public works in which the combined values of utility and aesthetics were paramount. He felt that parks and civic beautification would uplift and improve humanity, and subscribed to the City Beautiful movement. As a politician, his genius was to provide the political will and financing for public building and landscaping programs that greatly enhanced the areas in which they were implemented. He did this in a quiet, unostentatious fashion, which undoubtedly aided his goals; Canadians, like people elsewhere, do not suffer beauty readily. A man of remarkable vision, McQuesten did not seek personal gain, nor power for its own sake. He sought political power to indulge in his love of creating large and beautiful public works that would better the human condition. He felt personally obligated to use his privileges of birth and education for the social good.

In 1922 McQuesten was appointed by Hamilton City Council to the city's Board of Parks Management. He was the driving force behind a very ambitious program of parks acquisition by the BPM during the first decade of his tenure. He oversaw negotiations in the acquisition of Gage Park, and transformed Burlington Heights from an eyesore into a beautiful and grand entrance to the city. In the years 1927-31, Hamilton's park system nearly quadrupled through his capable and dynamic leadership.

Working behind the scenes in his usual fashion—in this case contributing his skills as a lawyer in putting together complicated deals—McQuesten was instrumental in attracting McMaster University (then a small Baptist university in Toronto) to Hamilton. He secured for the University a donation of 50 acres of land from a 400-acre parcel recently acquired by the BPM around Cootes Paradise, and offered landscaped grounds.

Having helped to attract the requisite university for the city, McQuesten then applied for and received permission from Buckingham Palace to establish a Royal Botanical Garden in Hamilton. And in the east end of the city, although the acquisition of the 700-acre Kings Forest Park was controversial because of cost, McQuesten persevered, convinced that East Hamilton deserved the same benefits as the western part of the city.

The first major assault on construction of a series of new mountain access roads was begun under his guidance. The Sherman Cut and the two east and west roads leading up to it were blasted out of the Escarpment face in the 1920's.

In the 1930's McQuesten served as Minister of Public Works and Minister of Highways in the Ontario Liberal Cabinet. Provincially, he was responsible for the construction of 4,000 miles of highways and three international bridges, including Niagara's Rainbow Bridge. As Chairman of the Niagara Parks Commission, he established a horticultural school and developed the stunning parks system around the Falls and along the length of the Niagara Parkway, which draws international admiration to this day.

Following the death of Thomas McQuesten from intestinal cancer at the beginning of 1948, Whitehern was donated to the city of Hamilton by bequest of his three surviving siblings. Located on a quiet street beside City Hall, the family home is preserved today as a museum, open to the public, along with an extensive archive of original documents that offer a unique view of Hamilton's past. This archival material was used by John Best for a biog-

Whitehern, the McQuesten family home, is preserved today as a museum with 19th century furnishings (including clothing) intact, offering the public a unique window onto Victorian life.

raphy of Thomas Baker McQuesten which focuses on his distinguished political career. The life of Mary Baker McQuesten is being brought more clearly to light through the work of scholar Mary Anderson, whose doctoral research at McMaster University offers insights into the literary and cultural aspects of the archival letters and written documents.

Whitehern was officially handed over to the city in 1968 following the death of the last surviving member of the family, Rev. Calvin McQuesten. With his passing, the family lineage (in keeping with Mrs. Baker's interventions) came to an end. However, the enduring legacy of Thomas B. McQuesten lives on as a testament to this exceptional family. His legacy stands, moreover, among Hamilton's—and Ontario's—finest accomplishments.

By the late 1920's, this old iron bridge needed to be replaced. The Board of Parks Management suggested a four-lane bridge, twice the normal width for such a bridge at that time. A number of budget-conscious councillors objected, but the wider bridge eventually won out. Four 40-foot Art Deco towers to be faced in limestone quarried from the Escarpment proved to be more contentious. The mayor and the Board of Control voted to build the bridge without the towers to save money; but following much pro-tower lobbying orchestrated in part by T. B. McQuesten, the Council as a whole voted for them.

The replacement of the old bridge by a handsome new one which would become a symbol for Hamilton, illustrates well the nature of McQuesten's contributions. Working behind the scenes, he was able in many circumstances to raise the aesthetic level of a project and then manipulate the political process to achieve its realisation.

The handsome McQuesten High Level Bridge serves as a gateway to Hamilton from the northwest. Niches in each of its four towers were designed to hold statues of important figures in Hamilton's history, but disagreements over who should be so honoured prevented this concept from being completed.

During the debates over the new bridge in 1930, the *Hamilton Spectator* published this editorial in support of the towers:

"In one moment the board of control dissipates the dreams of cultured Hamiltonians. In a high tone, a tone almost of moral indignation, it orders the removal of these artistic appendages. A bridge is a bridge, what more should it be? We imagine the controllers thinking. What matters if it be flat, drab, uninteresting, so long as it carries traffic? But bridges have to be looked at as well as driven over. And what a fine monument it will be to the 1931 board of control when, some time in the future, it stands out mean and incongruous against a background of beauty, like a wart on a pretty woman's chin."

The original pre-Depression plans for the northwest entry to the city called for numerous structures such as entrance gates and a plaza with a seven-storey obelisk, along with other buildings such as gas stations, a restaurant, a zoo, among other things. With the coming of the Depression the architectural structures were cut, and the entrance to the city retained a more natural look which has been maintained to this day.

The swings of economic fortunes, the outcomes of political debates, the presence of a certain individual at a particular time can each play a significant role in determining the appearance and fate of a city for many years to come.

Two bridges across the Desjardins Canal are seen here. The railroad bridge is the lower of the two, the upper or high level bridge being for road use.

Both bridges had an eventful life. Not long after this image was crafted, the high level suspension bridge was blown over during a windstorm. The railway bridge was later the scene of the famous Desjardins Canal Disaster of 1857 in which 59 people were killed. A passenger train from Toronto broke an axle while crossing the bridge, and

the engine fell onto the bridge which collapsed under the impact. It was unbelievably bad luck. Had the axle broken anywhere else along the route from Toronto, the carnage would have been much less. The structure which collapsed was a swing bridge, allowing it to be moved when high-masted schooners came through the canal cut; hence it was lighter and not as strong as a permanent bridge would have been.

The Rock Garden, pictured here in spring when the tulips are out, was once a worked-out gravel pit and is now part of the Royal Botanical Garden's 1,200-hectare (3,000-acre) holdings. It is situated on the ridge of land called Burlington Heights, which separates Cootes Paradise from the Bay. About 10,000 tons of Escarpment rock were trucked in from the Red Hill Creek Valley and the Waterdown area to create the rockery framework; this type of work was well-suited to being a relief project during the early years of the Depression, when it was constructed. This Garden brought international acclaim to Hamilton upon its completion.

The Urquhart Butterfly Garden, Canada's first municipal butterfly garden, is located in Dundas overlooking the former "Turning Basin" at the terminus of the Desjardins Canal. The concept was conceived when a rare giant swallowtail butterfly deposited an egg on a plant in the small natural garden at Chapman Books. The project came to fruition following several years of planning and fund raising by owner Joanna Chapman and a small group of other volunteers. The garden is named in honour of butterfly researchers Fred and Norah Urquhart, whose long years of dedicated research solved the mystery of monarch butterfly migration. It provides ideal habitat for numerous butterfly species, and includes host plantings to nurture larvae and nectar sources to feed the adults. It also features an educational kiosk. This Butterfly Garden is an inspiring example of what a handful of individuals can accomplish.

The covered walkway across King Street links the Jackson Square rooftop garden with the Art Gallery of Hamilton and the Irving Zucker Sculpture Court. Beyond the walkway is the Ellen Fairclough Building, which houses a multitude of provincial government offices. Its name honours a distinguished Hamiltonian who had an active career in civic and federal politics. Ms. Fairclough was named Secretary of State for Canada in 1957, thereby becoming the country's first federal woman cabinet minister. She subsequently served as Postmaster General, then as Minister of Citizenship and Immigration.

The Art Gallery of Hamilton, viewed here from King and Bay Streets, presents a handsome profile. Hamilton Place is glimpsed beyond; and a business tower rises in the distance.

Central Collegiate Institute (left) was completed in 1897. Originally both a high school and a teachers' college, by 1908 it functioned solely as a high school. The unusually handsome building was designed by young Hamilton architect Walter Stewart, who was only 24 at the time. It burned down in 1946.

Hamilton's "old" City Hall (right) was built in 1889, and demolished in 1961. Like the high school above, it had a Romanesque facade which was in vogue at the turn of the century for structures that required a dignified appearance.

Hamilton experienced periods of very rapid growth at the turn of the century. Already by the 1920's, the old city hall was being outgrown. This, coupled with the structural deterioration that was taking place, meant that the building would eventually have to be replaced. By the 1950's, the city was prepared to act. A decision was made to move to a new site; this would be the last city hall to be built beside the farmers' market. As is the case with most major decisions of this nature, a lively debate ensued over where to locate the new building. Sites ranging from across the road in the Lister Building, to the Westdale dump were suggested before the location on Main Street West was chosen. The land on which this building stood was sold to Eaton's.

Hamilton market in the mid-1800's, when it was an open-air meeting place

Since the 1830's, Hamilton has had a farmers' market that has been considered one of Canada's finest. At first it was an open area filled with a jumble of stands and sheds. It was both a retail outlet and a wholesale distribution centre. Animals were herded into town and slaughtered and butchered on the spot, with a rather casual approach to the blood, guts, stench and flies that accompany such activities.

A large Victorian brick structure was built in the late 1880's to house the vendors. It too, suffered from a lack of proper hygiene, especially with regards to the sanitary butchering of meat—a problem that was not

solved until fairly late. When the structure burned down in 1917, waves of rats where seen running from the doomed building. The old Victorian structure was replaced by long sheds with corrugated metal roofs, which many older readers will remember.

By the late 1950's, this land had become too valuable to remain in use as an open-air market. The land was built upon, and

The market in 1893, when this Victorian building was in use.

the market temporarily occupied the ground level of a parking ramp. Now it is housed in the basement level of the library complex (see next page).

The market in the 1950's

The main entrance to Hamilton Public Library (Central Branch). The farmers' market, located underground in the basement level of the library building, is accessible through separate entrances. When Hamilton was a much smaller pedestrian and streetcar city, the market was a vital link in the distribution of food from the surrounding farms to the urban dweller. With the arrival of the automobile, the central market place lost much of its importance since people could travel where they wished for their groceries, and wholesale facilities relocated elsewhere. Today the farmers' market is only one of many retail food outlets. Ironically, it had its greatest value when its state of cleanliness, hygiene and comfort level left something to be desired by today's standards.

"The Librarian" ("Il Biblio tecaro") graces the main entrance to the Hamilton Public Library. Created in 1911 by Angelo Biancini, the elegant statue was donated by the Italian citizens of Hamilton. Copps Coliseum is visible in the background.

Gage Park was purchased from the Gage family in 1918. The park was designed to include a formal garden, part of which is shown here. Thomas McQuesten wished to rename some of Hamilton's parks after historic figures. Wabasso Park had been changed to LaSalle Park, and he wished to call Gage Park after Sir Issac Brock, a hero of the War of 1812. The Gage family, which had done very nicely in the sale of their farmland to the city, offered to contribute to erecting this memorial fountain if the Gage name would be retained. The city fathers were persuaded.

Large areas of Gage Park are open spaces that have been planted with a variety of trees. In the background are greenhouses where a chrysanthemum show is held annually. Also nearby are a bandstand, and a tennis and a lawn bowling club. This park of approximately 64 acres is a carefully tended urban open space, in contrast to the much wilder areas of the Red Hill Creek and Dundas Valleys.

The Desjardins Canal, linking Dundas with Burlington Bay, was completed in 1837. The early merchants of Dundas had always dreamed of such a link. Expecting Dundas to flourish upon its completion, numbers of businessmen invested in the town while the canal was being built. Among others, the Gartshore iron foundry (founded in 1838) would likely not have come to Dundas had it not been for the new canal. However, the waterway itself never achieved its expectations in terms of cargo volumes, coming as it did after Hamilton's harbour had been opened up and only shortly before the railways came, siphoning off trade from the town's hinterland. Today the Desjardins Canal is a peaceful waterway enjoyed by waterfowl and people in canoes.

LaSalle Park Marina, in Burlington. A large Great Lakes shipping vessel and Hamilton's steel mills lie across the Bay, shrouded in morning mist. In 1820, Brown's Wharf was built here to handle products from the Aldershot and Waterdown areas. Flour, wood for lake steamers, and fruits and vegetables were shipped from this location. In the late 1800's the area became a popular park and amusement area for family outings and for organised company events. Part of the thrill was a boat ride across the Bay to and from the docks around James Street. Originally called Wabasso Park, the name was changed in the 1920's to LaSalle Park to honour the first European explorer who passed through this area in the 1660's. Sailing yachts on the Bay has been popular for more than a century, and the first yacht club, which no longer exists, was established in Hamilton in the 1870's.

St. John's Anglican Church in Ancaster is a good example of late Gothic Revival architecture, and one of many buildings in the Hamilton area which is recognised under the Ontario Heritage Act as historically significant. This handsome structure was built from local stone after the original wooden church burned in 1868. The wooden structure, erected in 1824, was initially a "free" church shared by Anglicans and Presbyterians; it was consecrated solely for Anglican services in 1830. Tombstones, including many that date from the 19th century, shelter peacefully among magnificent oaks in the lovely church cemetery.

McMaster Divinity College is modern in appearance (its cornerstone was laid in 1959), but the cloisters on the other side of the building give it a medieval touch. When McMaster University became non-denominational in 1957 to gain access to public funding, the Divinity College became a separately incorporated institution on campus that retains the function of theological education in the Baptist faith. William McMaster, an Irish immigrant who lived from 1811 to 1887, was instrumental in founding both the Canadian Imperial Bank of Commerce and McMaster University. He wished to further Baptist education, and left a large estate for this purpose. In 1887, the Toronto Baptist College and another Baptist institution were merged to form McMaster University. While the University now has gone its own way, the Divinity College retains the ties to Baptist learning that were so dear to William McMaster.

"Touchdown," a familiar feature of the downtown landscape, does not look out of place in a light snowfall. The dynamic sculpture stands at the entrance to the Canadian Football Hall of Fame and Museum situated beside City Hall. It is fitting that Hamilton, with its strong tradition of Tiger Cat football, was chosen as the location for this institution. Hamilton Place is in the background.

McMaster University Arts Quadrangle during a gentle snowfall. The welded steel sculpture was created in 1973 by a member of the Fine Arts Department, G. B. Wallace. He entitled it "Man Releasing Eagles" and left the interpretation to the viewer. The eagle is found in McMaster's coat of arms and other University emblems, and symbolises a heavenly vision.

King Street East is seen here from just past Gore Park in the city's centre. First Place is the imposing structure on the south side of the street.

The elegant stone spire of St. Paul's Presbyterian Church (see page 7) rises in Gothic Revival splendour between the rear entrance to City Hall (foreground) and the Century 21 building.

The Red Hill Creek Valley in the east end of Hamilton is one of the largest urban green spaces in Canada. It is also the subject of an excellent new book edited by Walter G. Peace of McMaster University's Geography Department. *From Mountain to Lake: The Red Hill Creek Valley* looks at the Valley from several different perspectives, illustrating the historical evolution and present character of its natural, cultural and political landscape.

Red Hill Creek takes its name from the red hills which are prominent features in portions of its valley. The reddish colouring comes from iron in the shales of the bedrock formation, exposed on bluffs and hills adjacent to the creek bed. The 700-acre King's Forest purchased by the City of Hamilton in 1929 is located in the Red Hill Creek Valley.

A much-debated freeway is planned to be built in the Valley, connecting with a recently completed limited-access road that traverses the length of the "Mountain." At the time of writing, the future course of events was not yet clear.

Spencer Creek, shown here, flows over the brow of the Niagara Escarpment at Webster's Falls. This view into Spencer Gorge is from the top of the Falls. The Gorge was cut deeply into the Niagara Escarpment during the retreat of the Pleistocene glaciers. Massive torrents of glacial meltwater loaded with abrasive sand and rock poured from the north, in the process cutting the spectacular twin-armed gorge into the north wall of the Dundas Valley, to the west of Hamilton.

The Hamilton Region Conservation Area owns Spencer Gorge, along with several acres of land around it. The Bruce Trail passes through the Gorge and is just at the right of the stream in this photo.

The Dundas Valley with its rolling and forested topography has provided a rural setting for numbers of wealthy individuals who value living on a secluded country estate. While some estates are also found in the Red Hill Creek Valley, the latter never developed the same clustering of estate properties that occurred in the Dundas Valley, especially in parts of Ancaster (seen here). The Tamahaac Club, a watering hole of the local upper crust, is also found along the wooded slopes of this portion of the Dundas Valley.

A rather closely knit gentry emerged from within this group. Being of British background, possessing mannerisms and tastes which emulated upper class Britain, they felt strong ties of loyalty to the Mother Country, and service in the military during the Wars was expected. Constant rounds of socialising were a hallmark of this group.

The back of City Hall presents a soft face during a light snowfall.

This rail yard was constructed in the early 1850's, and was for many decades the centre of rail transportation for Hamilton. Now it functions as a marshalling yard for the CNR. While there are no immediate plans for the CN to relocate these yards to the suburbs, it is likely that someday this will happen, leaving these lands free for use as public open space or residential development.

Plans have been made to build a wide asphalt path, similar to that in the photo on page 45, along the edge of the Bay to Princess Point in Cootes Paradise. The CN has sold a narrow strip of land along the water's edge to the City of Hamilton to make this possible. A floating bridge will take the trail through the Desjardins Canal. People will then be able to walk, bicycle and skate from the new bayfront parks to the marshes and the Westdale area in a beautiful natural setting.

This old Victorian red brick building was Hamilton's station during the heyday of the railway era.

The Stuart Street Customs House was built in the mid-1850's, when the railway and harbour were an important shipping centre. It is now the Ontario Workers' Arts and Heritage Centre.

Hamilton for many years lobbied Ottawa for a new railroad terminal, not only for reasons of functionality but as a symbol of the city's vitality and progressiveness. As fate would have it, when this structure was at last completed in 1933, the age of railway passenger travel was soon to end. The building's use as a terminal gradually diminished, and by the early 90's it had become vacant. A new tenant is now being sought who will renovate the structure.

In addition to being an important docking area, the rail yard at the turn of the 20th century was the cradle of heavy industry for the city of Hamilton. A rolling mill and other metalworking facilities had evolved from the factories originally established to service the railways.

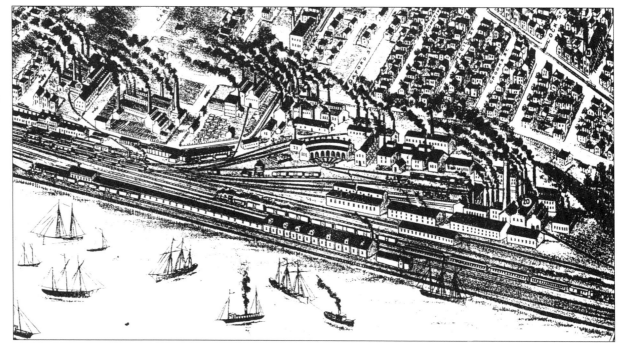

In 1939 the city's mayor stated, "I have always said that Hamilton couldn't have both the greatest industrial harbour in Canada and bathing beaches in close proximity. The council has to ask itself if it is more important to have our industries or our bathing beach in the bay."

With improvements in technology, it is now possible to have both swimming and industry in the Bay. Not only has industry greatly reduced its level of pollution, but the City of Hamilton has made a major effort to limit the amount of untreated storm runoff by constructing huge concrete tanks to hold rain water until it can be treated at the sewage treatment plant.

There has long been a separation of the city from its waterfront for Hamilton citizens. The waterfront along the Bay was traditionally viewed only as a place for shipping and industry. Some people managed to find informal swimming spots in between the factories and docks, but until the end of WWI no location was set aside for public swimming. The few places that did open after the War were soon closed, due to increasing pollution. Now an effort is being made to make the waterfront accessible to the public: to bring the downtown psychologically closer to the Bay. Most large cities with waterfronts have provided public access to them, enhancing the quality of life for their citizens. Part of the greatness of cities such as London and Vancouver has been pedestrian access to their waters. Hamilton has been an exception to this approach, and now positive steps are being taken to reverse the situation.

Countless people pass by these three large tombs in the Hamilton Cemetery as they walk in Dundurn Park or drive in and out of Hamilton. These are the final resting places of three successful Hamilton businessmen who died at the turn of the 20th century. The tomb on the far left belongs to George Tuckett, and the one in the centre to Thomas Watkins. The exceptionally attractive above-ground granite mausoleum was built by William E. Sanford. The mound of earth on which the tombs stand was part of the defensive ramparts constructed by the British Army to protect troops billeted here against any invading American armies during the War of 1812.

George Tuckett made his money in tobacco and had a large factory on Queen Street North. It is said that during the American Civil War when Confederate tobacco was not available here, he went down to Virginia, into Confederate territory, and purchased what he needed. When the battlefront pushed south he came back, and was able to supply the locals with plug tobacco. Tuckett built a Romanesque "pile" on a ridge of land (a continuation of the same gravel bar on which the High Level Bridge is situated) that overlooks the town and the Bay. This higher land was chosen by numbers of wealthy individuals as a desirable place to live. Following his death in 1900, the structure remained vacant for a number of years until it was purchased by the Scottish Rite, and a major addition was put on.

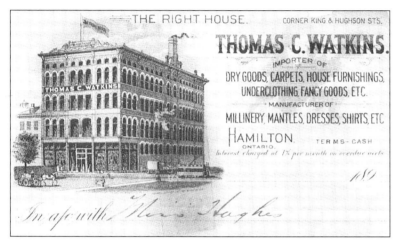

The Right House, completed in 1893, was Hamilton's first major department store. An unusually attractive building, it has been a Hamilton landmark for over a century. Its owner, Thomas C. Watkins, had been in the retail business since 1843, and this building became the symbol of his success. The original structure (a dry goods store) was modified by Watkins without having to close the business down. The four-storey structure with large plate glass windows and massive polished granite columns was designed to impress a wealthy clientele.

William E. Sanford was a wealthy industrialist who at his prime employed over 2,000 people making ready-to-wear clothing in a huge factory at King and John Streets. He also served for a time as a Senator in the federal government. His mansion, located on a city block of land on the same hump-backed ridge as the Tuckett home, was built at the beginning of the last decade of the 19th century. In Victorian times this area was on the outskirts of town, and large lots with gardens tended by servants were still possible. The housewarming party in 1892 was a spectacle of social grandeur, with more than a thousand of the "right" people attending.

Sanford accidentally drowned in 1899, but his widow lived to be 90, dying in 1938. A number of wealthy, socially prominent widows like Mrs. Sanford maintained their Victorian homes and lifestyles on huge, fenced-in properties well into the 20th century, long after that era had ended. Within a year of Mrs. Sanford's death the house was torn down to make room for a subdivision of one-storey houses centred on a street named for the original property—Wesanford.

The fountain at the front entrance to City Hall is especially attractive when the surrounding flower beds are in full bloom.

Approaching the front entrance to City Hall from Bay Street, one passes by the evocative statue by William Epp entitled "Migration."

The gardens at the rear of City Hall are glorious in spring when the magnolias are in bloom. Along with the nearby gardens at Whitehern, they provide an area of quiet away from downtown Hamilton's busy streets.

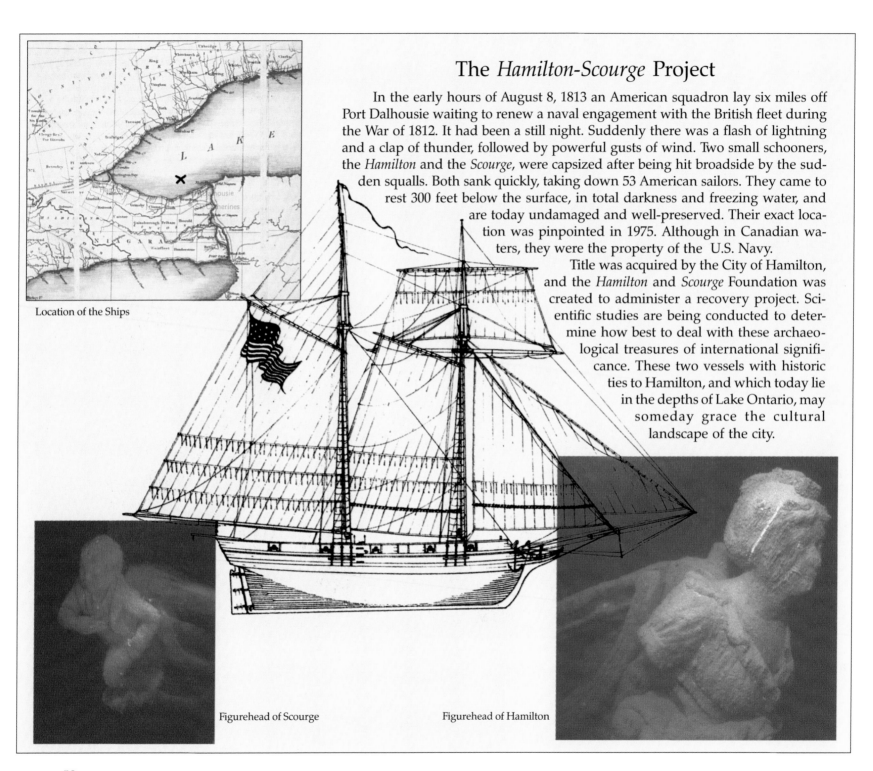

The *Hamilton-Scourge* Project

In the early hours of August 8, 1813 an American squadron lay six miles off Port Dalhousie waiting to renew a naval engagement with the British fleet during the War of 1812. It had been a still night. Suddenly there was a flash of lightning and a clap of thunder, followed by powerful gusts of wind. Two small schooners, the *Hamilton* and the *Scourge*, were capsized after being hit broadside by the sudden squalls. Both sank quickly, taking down 53 American sailors. They came to rest 300 feet below the surface, in total darkness and freezing water, and are today undamaged and well-preserved. Their exact location was pinpointed in 1975. Although in Canadian waters, they were the property of the U.S. Navy.

Title was acquired by the City of Hamilton, and the *Hamilton* and *Scourge* Foundation was created to administer a recovery project. Scientific studies are being conducted to determine how best to deal with these archaeological treasures of international significance. These two vessels with historic ties to Hamilton, and which today lie in the depths of Lake Ontario, may someday grace the cultural landscape of the city.

Location of the Ships

Figurehead of Scourge

Figurehead of Hamilton

The Crooks Hollow ruins in West Flamborough are all that remain of one of Canada's earliest industrial centres. In the decades after the War of 1812, an industrial complex was organised here by Scottish entrepreneur James Crooks that utilised the water power of Spencer Creek (seen flowing past the mill wall). A wide range of enterprises, from the usual grist and saw mills to a cooperage, a distillery and a brewery, were established. Under Crooks' initiative, the first paper mill in Canada was located here as well. The legislature of Upper Canada had offered a sizeable prize to anyone who would build a paper mill, and Crooks was able to beat out the competition.

With the coming of the railways to Hamilton in the mid-1850's, and the use of steam power, Crooks Hollow declined as an industrial centre and today is a unique and charming little nook near Greensville.

The Crooks family not only owned land and mills; they also possessed a schooner named the *Lord Nelson*. Two weeks prior to the outbreak of the War of 1812, U.S. Naval authorities seized the schooner in American waters off the south shore of Lake Ontario on suspicion of smuggling. When war was declared a few weeks later, the U.S. Navy purchased, commissioned and armed the ship, renaming it the *Scourge*. This vessel, along with an American schooner, subsequently sank in a sudden squall near St.Catharines. After the war, the Crooks brothers sought compensation. The American courts declared the seizure illegal and awarded compensation. By a series of quirks, it was more than one hundred years before a pittance was finally paid out in 1930.

The gateway to Hamilton harbour, the Burlington Bay Canal was opened in 1832. It gave Hamilton direct access to Lake Ontario and made the young community a chief port of call for lake schooners and steamers. The channel into Burlington Bay must occasionally be dredged to counteract ongoing silting.

At one time the piers were built of wood, which habitually caught fire from embers ejected from the smokestacks of wood-fired steamers.

These graves in Woodland Cemetery are reserved for military veterans who served in Canada's armed forces. Their simple but strong patterns create a powerful image of order.

The bell tower at the Eaton Centre is an attractive new addition to the downtown Hamilton landscape.

The glass facade of the Commerce Building reflects patterns of its surroundings at the corner of James and King Streets. The Canadian Imperial Bank of Commerce and McMaster University were both founded by William McMaster, who left his mark on Hamilton indirectly and in a fashion that he could not have imagined in his lifetime. (See page 33)

Summer's Lane provides access to downtown Hamilton's major arts and entertainment complex. It was named after theatre promoter Harry Summers, who had a theatre on the Mountain at the top of the Wentworth incline between the years of 1902-1914.

The Toronto, Hamilton and Buffalo Railway terminal was recently renovated and is now the city's bus and Go station. Both the CNR station (see page 43) and the TH&B station were built at approximately the same time in the early 1930's. The CNR station used classical forms from the past, whereas the TH&B station adopted new styling that was fashionable at the time.

This building can be considered an amalgam of Art Moderne in its broad outlines, with Art Deco decorative touches. The smooth wall finish, with windows flush to the surface, was used to create a streamlined effect that symbolised speed—a theme common in the arts at the time. The repetition of geometric shapes at the top of the tower is a characteristic Art Deco decorative device. The bus terminal shelter is post-Modern.

The rail tracks lie at a higher elevation than the roadways that surround the station. The railway bed was raised in 1931 as a Depression relief project, ending more than twenty years of serious disruption to street traffic by the endless comings and goings of trains. Only a grade separation could solve the problem.

The CN tracks climbing out of the Dundas Valley were built almost 150 years ago by the Great Western Railroad. They gave Hamilton dominance over its rival communities of Dundas and Ancaster in the struggle for commercial supremacy in this area. In this section they abut picturesque conservation areas.

Along with slow freight trains, these tracks are used by Via passenger trains. The latter come downhill at high speeds with minimal engine power, giving little warning time for unwary trespassers on the tracks. Deer mesmerized by train lights are occasionally cut cleanly in half by a speeding train.

Wooden stairs around 1870.

Beckett Drive at the turn of the century.

One outcome of the coming of electricity at the turn of the century was the construction of a local electric railway network, centred on Hamilton, that radiated out to Oakville, Beamsville, Brantford and Dundas. This short-distance radial network operated for a period of forty years—from 1891 to 1931, at which time competition from motor vehicles made it uneconomical. Here we see the Hamilton-to-Brantford radial car ascending the Escarpment.

Travelling along a modern-day access route up the Niagara Escarpment, few drivers are aware that they are passing through 400 million years of geologic history in their climb or descent of the Mountain. This road begins its descent from Upper James Street.

Wooden stairs up the Escarpment have existed for over a century. It is only in the last decade that galvanised steel stairs have supplanted them. These stairs are very heavily used. One way of telling how long they have been in use is to notice whether the railings have become smooth and glassy from the many, sweaty hands that have handled them.

Abandoned rail lines have been converted into trails along the Escarpment.

The Gore 1861

The triangular shape of Gore Park in the city centre is the unintended inspiration of George Hamilton, for whom the city is named. He owned a triangular piece of land which he hoped to combine with a similar piece owned by Nathaniel Hughson to form a rectangular town square. The deal with Hughson fell through, and Hamilton acquired its distinctive town centre by default.

For a number of years, the town council wished to build on the Gore's open land, and only the vigorous efforts of local citizens preserved it as open space. It remained unkempt until 1860, serving as a parking area for horse-drawn vehicles. The occasion of the city's first royal visit prompted the town council to turn it into a park. Having created a park, council then fenced it off and for over a decade in the 1870's and 80's kept citizens out. Initially, the park extended only from James to Hughson and wasn't extended to John Street for another forty years.

The Gore 1870's

60

Looking south on James Street from Eaton Centre, the "Mountain" is seen clearly in the distance. Gore Park, in the centre of the city, is two blocks ahead on the left.

The Escarpment, with its rolling hills and generally rugged topography, provides an ideal setting for golf courses. The Glendale Golf and Country Club pictured here is a private club in the Red Hill Creek Valley.

On the other side of Hamilton, in the Dundas Valley, this private club is known as the Dundas Golf and Curling Club.

An elevated walkway carries pedestrians above the floodplain of Grindstone Creek, which flows through Waterdown and enters the Bay near Valley Inn Road. The walkway provides a special way to experience a marsh, and has allowed badly trampled marsh vegetation to restore itself to a lush state. Much work has also been done to restore fish habitat in this watershed.

This quiet spot frequented by fishermen, and the site of a quaint and noisy single-lane wooden bridge, was once a busy transportation node. It was also the natural outlet from Cootes Paradise before the Desjardins Canal cut was made, at which time this outlet was filled in for transportation purposes. Barges carrying goods to and from Dundas would be poled through here, and an important road link from Hamilton to Burlington also passed by. At this busy confluence of routes, the Valley Inn Hotel was built around 1850. When the water and road networks shifted location the inn fell into disuse, and in the late 1920's it was damaged by fire and eventually demolished.

McMaster University lends a distinction to Hamilton that comes with a centre of higher learning. Its cultured atmosphere and beautiful campus include this cloistered island of peace and calm by the archway between University Hall and Edwards Hall.

T. B. McQuesten commented after Hamilton had succeeded in attracting McMaster: "… we've never landed such a fish as this… Our whole development has been along mechanics lines. And the result has been, the owners don't live here… and Hamilton has become too much a factory town. This is the first break toward a broader culture and a higher educational development. It was sorely needed."

McMaster University's athletic building is a prominent and distinctive structure on the campus. The athletic grounds to the rear of this building are nestled among ravines of the Dundas Valley and give one the feeling of being on the grounds of an exclusive school in England.

A pleasure enjoyed by numbers of Hamilton residents is walking on the beautiful grounds of McMaster University. Numerous trees not native to the area have been planted on the campus, and can be a challenge to identify.

Gore Park is located in the centre of Hamilton, at King and James Streets. A notable feature of the city from early on (see page 60), it underwent a major facelift a decade ago. Some components, however, remain unchanged.

In 1901, a few days after Queen Victoria's death, a group of socially prominent women decided to honour her memory with a statue. A committee was formed, money raised and a competition organised for the best design. In the spring of 1908, a large crowd of over 20,000 witnessed the unveiling of the bronze statue that has become one of Hamilton's landmarks. It is now regularly washed and waxed to protect it from birds and the elements.

The bronze statue of Sir John A. Macdonald was erected in 1893 and stands a little over eight feet tall, atop a granite pedestal. Sir John's national policy, which imposed high tariffs on manufactured goods, led to a rapid growth of Hamilton industries—in part from the influx of American subsidiaries seeking to avoid the duties. His policies of national railway building and encouraging settlement of the West led to an increase in demand for products that Hamilton produced. Local business leaders appreciative of his leadership helped to fund the statue. Although not a resident of the city, Macdonald played an important role in Hamilton's industrial development. The cenotaph behind Sir John was put up in 1923 to honour Hamilton's war dead.

A reporter in 1859 wrote, "To erect a public fountain is a work of charity and mercy, a moral and a virtuous act. It cannot be misapplied, it can never become obsolete."

The original Gore Park fountain, privately funded, was put in place in 1861 and lasted a century. The one seen in this picture is its replacement, completed in 1970. The splendid large red-and-buff structure across the road is the former Right House department store (see page 47).

In the distance, numerous office towers and apartment blocks that sprang up in Hamilton after WWII spread across the horizon. The stone house in the foreground dates back to a more leisurely period, when wealthy Hamiltonians built sumptuous homes at the well-drained base of the Niagara Escarpment. Limestone quarried from the Escarpment was used to build this particular house.

Close to Albion Falls is a charming little waterfall known as Buttermilk Falls. It has steeper, more enclosed sides than Albion Falls, and has quite a different feel, but still has the "look" of a classic Escarpment landform.

Hamilton's steel mills (in this case Stelco) possess a majesty of their own. Here, within the white-hot cauldrons of the blast furnaces, iron is liberated from the rock in which it was formed many millions of years ago.

These blast furnaces are part of the Dofasco iron and steel complex. The harbour facilities seen in both pictures make it possible to bring in cheaply the huge amounts of raw material required in the steel-making process.

"The Beach is like a park covered with large spreading Oaks."

Sketch and comment by Lady Simcoe, *circa* 1790

The beach strip is a narrow bar of sand about four miles long that separates Lake Ontario (right) from Burlington Bay (left). The building in the picture is the King's Head Inn—a two-storey frame government inn and military storage depot. It had a short life. Built in 1794, it was burned to the ground by an American naval flotilla in 1813, during the War of 1812. Further up this sand bar, a British naval unit was saved by a fluke occurrence from the very real prospect of being annihilated by a larger American naval force. The inlet into Burlington Bay was normally quite shallow, and even small warships were unable to pass through. On this occasion there was a strong easterly wind which piled up the water and allowed the British ships, which were being pursed by the American force, to slip into the Bay to safety. This particular pursuit is known today as "The Burlington Races," and it allowed the British fleet to maintain an important strategic presence on Lake Ontario during the rest of the War.

Because of its great distance from central Hamilton, development of the beach strip was limited until the building of the railway in 1876. The steam railway led to a number of luxury resorts opening up, with guests normally coming for an extended stay. While people came to enjoy the water and the beaches, it didn't hurt to have a bowling alley, billiard room, ballroom, tennis courts and other amenities handy.

When the electric radial railroad came in 1896, it in effect made the beach strip a suburb of Hamilton, and day visits to the beaches became possible. Summer cottages were built and permanent homes began to appear. In the early decades of the 20th century the resorts declined as areas like the Muskokas became more accessible.

The beach strip also became a fashionable area where wealthy Hamiltonians built large two-storey "cottages" in the 1890's, especially near the canal. When the yacht club erected this attractive Queen Anne club house in 1891, it became a summer focal point for the social life of the wealthy. The RHYC was the site of many balls, regattas and other social get-togethers. After a quarter of a century, this wooden structure burned down and the yacht club moved back to the area near the foot of James Street.

The beach strip falls along the shortest land route connecting Toronto to the Niagara Peninsula. It was destined to become a major transportation corridor. Today there are two major bridges crossing the canal. The concrete structure shown in the foreground was completed in 1985. Its twin, the steel arch bridge, is barely visible in the background. For years after the steel arch bridge was completed in 1958, tolls were collected. The bridge tolls served to divert traffic onto Beach Boulevard, which is the main road. When the tolls were removed, the boulevard reverted to a lightly-used residential street with generally little traffic except when the passage of a ship backs up cars at the canal. In portions of the beach strip there are sixteen lanes of roads: that is real progress.

Both these pictures of beach strip houses illustrate the distinctive architectural style of turn-of-the-century homes in this area. A number of houses of this style are clustered near the canal and have been restored at great expense. Most of the houses on the strip were built at a later period and have contemporary styles seen elsewhere in Hamilton. However the beach strip does have a unique ambience characterised by the merging of nature and industry.

The two bridges are a towering presence, and along with their approaches, generate an accompanying hum of traffic. The power lines along the Lake Ontario shore make a strong visual impact. The beauty of the Hamilton skyline with its steel mills can be seen across the waters of the Bay, and on the other side of the strip is the more pristine beauty of Lake Ontario with its sandy beach.

There are periods when high water levels on Lake Ontario produce serious flooding in this area. Black coal dust from the steel industries has darkened the skies and hearths of beach strip homes. Pollution of the waters has at times led to an accumulation of large numbers of dead fish on the shores of the strip. In the 1980's, plans were put forward to buy out the homes of the strip residents and turn the area into a nature preserve. But many of the beach strip owners did not want to move. The plans were dropped, and this most distinctive community lives on.

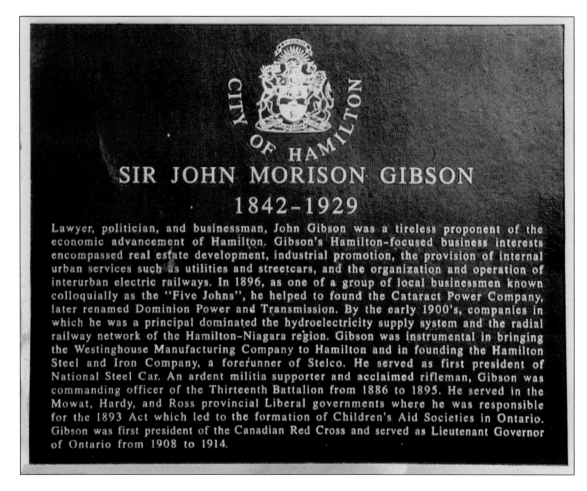

SIR JOHN MORISON GIBSON

1842-1929

Lawyer, politician, and businessman, John Gibson was a tireless proponent of the economic advancement of Hamilton. Gibson's Hamilton-focused business interests encompassed real estate development, industrial promotion, the provision of internal urban services such as utilities and streetcars, and the organization and operation of interurban electric railways. In 1896, as one of a group of local businessmen known colloquially as the "Five Johns", he helped to found the Cataract Power Company, later renamed Dominion Power and Transmission. By the early 1900's, companies in which he was a principal dominated the hydroelectricity supply system and the radial railway network of the Hamilton-Niagara region. Gibson was instrumental in bringing the Westinghouse Manufacturing Company to Hamilton and in founding the Hamilton Steel and Iron Company, a forerunner of Stelco. He served as first president of National Steel Car. An ardent militia supporter and acclaimed rifleman, Gibson was commanding officer of the Thirteenth Battalion from 1886 to 1895. He served in the Mowat, Hardy, and Ross provincial Liberal governments where he was responsible for the 1893 Act which led to the formation of Children's Aid Societies in Ontario. Gibson was first president of the Canadian Red Cross and served as Lieutenant Governor of Ontario from 1908 to 1914.

In the last several decades of this century, the computer has changed the world we live in. A hundred years ago electricity was the new wonder technology. Electric motors began to appear in factories, replacing steam boilers; and electrically driven streetcars replaced steam- and horse-powered vehicles for city use.

A number of unusually talented and aggressive business leaders in Hamilton at the turn of the last century took advantage of this new technology to further their own and Hamilton's fortunes. One such group was known as the "Five Johns" (an expression that probably would not be used today). Their plan was to bring electric power to Hamilton in order to strengthen and enlarge its industrial base, and also to establish a network of electrified commuter railways focused on Hamilton that would make the city the centre of its own commercial and industrial empire in southern Ontario.

Improvements to the Welland Canal completed in 1887 created an unusual opportunity for this group, which they quickly seized. A secondary canal had been built to provide the water to operate the locks through which ships passed. This canal carried more water than was required for the operation of the main canal. The "Five Johns" purchased the rights to this surplus water, built a hydro- electric plant on the Escarpment just west of St. Catharines, and transmitted the power to Hamilton. At the time it was an innovative and risky step, but it paid off. The cheap and reliable supply of electricity helped to draw companies like Westinghouse and Otis Elevator to the city, and was instrumental in the growth of manufacturing that took place. The personal links that local businessmen forged with American industrialists helped to encourage large companies to invest in the city, and made Hamilton the branch plant manufacturing capital of Canada at the turn of the century. The City of Hamilton itself offered tax subsidies, along with free land on which to build.

The most prominent of the "Five Johns" was John Gibson, skilled in the art of industrial promotion and real estate development. He also bought large holdings in the east of Hamilton when it was still farm land. When the need for residential land for workers' housing developed, he was in a position to supply it. As an important stockholder in the radial electric railroad, it was perhaps not a total coincidence that a newly built line passed through his property.

These inlets were once some of best spawning grounds on Lake Ontario. They have long since been filled in and are now part of the industrial complex of Hamilton.

Approximately twenty-five percent of Burlington Bay has been filled in.

This is one of three islands along the beach strip that have been created to provide habitat for birds such as the Caspian and common tern that nest together in colonies. These are ground-nesting species which can easily be disrupted by such predators as foxes. By giving them their own islands they can nest in safety. The birds in this photo are cormorants which are sitting on platforms attached to wooden poles. Underwater structures containing rocks that are configured to be conducive to the spawning of fish such as lake trout and whitefish have been built. These islands have been carefully researched and are of sophisticated ecological design.

A view of the Dofasco properties, whose massive shed-buildings, specialised equipment in the foreground, and blast furnaces in the background illustrate the appearance of Hamilton's industrial landscape.

Downtown Hamilton office buildings are seen across the roof of the newly constructed bus terminal in the foreground.

Copps Coliseum, named for former mayor Victor K. Copps, was built in 1985 and has a seating capacity of 18,000. A wide variety of events are held here and range from hockey games to celebrity events.

Hamilton Place, viewed from the front of City Hall, is internationally renowned for its acoustics and hosts a wide range of opera, theatre and concert performances. It houses a Great Hall, which is home for the New Hamilton Orchestra and for Opera Hamilton, and a small Studio Theatre. The Ellen Fairclough Building rises above it in the background.

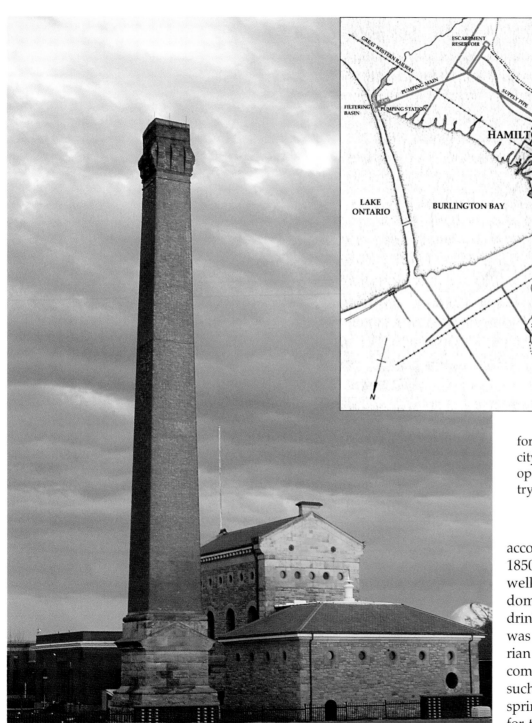

MAP OF HAMILTON'S FIRST WATER
SUPPLY SYSTEM IN 1856

Notice the appearance of Hamilton harbour before infilling took place. The location of the docks for the city was around the foot of James Street. The undeveloped south shore of the Bay would allow the steel industry to locate in Hamilton.

The Hamilton Pumping Station was a major accomplishment of mid-19th century Hamilton. By the 1850's Hamilton's water supply, which came from wells, was no longer adequate. Both industrial and domestic pollution were making the water unfit to drink, and cholera—a horrible waterborne disease—was taking its grim toll. Fires, a scourge of the Victorian city, could not be fought with the limited supply coming from wells. The city considered all the options, such as drawing water from Burlington Bay, or from springs of the Escarpment. The only solution feasible for the long run was chosen, even though it was the

most costly one: water would be drawn from Lake Ontario and pumped into the city. Sewage would flow into the Bay. This, by the way, is the pattern of flow to this day and will likely remain as such. With time, however, sewage has received more and more treatment and is less of a pollutant.

A large basin, 16 feet deep and three football fields long, was dug near the shore of Lake Ontario. Water percolating from the lake was filtered by sand and then pumped to a reservoir part way up the Escarpment in the Kenilworth-Ottawa area. From here it flowed by gravity along Main Street to James. The steam-driven pumping equipment came from the Gartshore Foundry in Dundas.

The pump house had an Italian Chapel facade, and the chimney was built to a height of 150 feet which also served as a naviga-tion aid to ships on the Lake. The pump house has 3-foot-thick limestone walls and 3″ white oak floors.

In 1910 the city installed new pumps powered by electricity, but the steam equipment was retained as a backup until 1938, at which time it went out of use. The pump house with its attached boiler room then remained vacant until the 1970's, when both were restored. Opened to the public in 1983, this structure (now the Hamilton Museum of Steam and Technology) is quite a beauty and well worth seeing. It is the only example of its kind in North America.

A series of concrete reservoirs in which water is stored for city use have been built along the edge of the Mountain brow. These massive containers are covered over and have grass fields on top which are often used for athletic purposes.

Sam Lawrence Park is named after a former labour leader and mayor. This well-known park is located just above the centre of the city at the top of the Jolley Cut, with a panoramic view of both the downtown and the steel mills. It has been designed for mass use, with parking conveniently close by, and easy-to-use paths. The underlying rock of the Escarpment has been integrated into the design of the flowerbeds, and an excellent interpretive display illustrates the geological configuration of this landform.

Dundas Peak is another prominent feature of the Escarpment, this time in the suburbs west of Hamilton. While not a formal park, it is owned by the regional Conservation Authority and is open to the public. Accessibility here is at the opposite pole of Sam Lawrence Park. A walk of several kilometres is entailed from the nearest parking, along a trail which is kept as natural as possible and has some sheer drops. Hikers and groups of teenagers are the major users.

Conservation lands in the Dundas Valley are extensive and superb. Earlier it was seen that the Board of Parks Management was responsible for acquiring a great deal of land early in this century that now constitutes an important part of Hamilton's parkland. A second period of public land acquisition on a large scale took place in the late 1960's and the 1970's, when the Hamilton Region Conservation Authority purchased sizeable properties in the rolling hills of the Dundas Valley. The Department of Highways had planned to put a major road through these hills, and a number of the earliest purchases were made to block this plan.

The Dundas Valley Conservation Area has one of the largest Carolinian forests remaining in Canada, and boasts an amazing range and variety of plant and animal species. An extensive trail system allows the public to explore its natural riches.

A trail in the Dundas Valley has a touch of magic after a light sprinkling of snow.

Downtown Hamilton at Main and MacNab, looking toward the Ellen Fairclough Building and, to the left of it, the rear entrance of Hamilton Place.

Centenary Methodist Church on Main Street just west of James is now known as Centenary United Church. It was given the name "centenary" to commemorate the one hundredth anniversary of the beginnings of Methodism in North America. This church with a distinctive Romanesque facade was completed in 1868 and renovated in the early 1920's. The deceptively modest exterior belies a large well-furnished structure that can seat about 1,300 people.

The Cathedral of Christ the King was built during the early years of the Depression—1931 to 1933. This was a very short period of time when compared to the decades of actual construction time that the European Cathedrals required. Given the depth of pocket book and the time horizon of the Catholic Church, the Depression was a good time to build, because the construction industry was slow and building costs were low.

The Cathedral was built upon a former cemetery from which the bodies had been removed for reburial in the Catholic cemetery on the north side of the Bay. This gateway to Westdale was intended to be a showplace. The beauty of the site has been diminished with the construction of Highway 403, which follows the valley of Chedoke Creek.

McMaster University Medical Centre, now referred to as the Hamilton Health Sciences Corporation, was officially opened in 1972. The mass of this major teaching hospital and children's hospital, now softened by mature trees, replaced the elegant low-profile Sunken Garden (inset) of the University's earlier days.

Artificially created islands and reefs dot the north side of the Bay. The vast fish-spawning grounds on the south side of the Bay were lost due to industrial infilling and pollution during the past century. These tiny spawning reefs, while a far cry from the original grounds, are part of an effort to improve the fish habitat. In the distance is the Canada Centre for Inland Waters (a massive federal government building), established for the purpose of improving the quality of the Bay's water.

This wealthy suburb on the north side of Burlington Bay looks out onto the steel mills across the water. LaSalle Park is just to the left of the picture. Only in Hamilton can such a photograph be taken.

Dundurn Castle

Dundurn Castle was built by Sir Alan MacNab, and was named after the area in Scotland from which his ancestors came. A man of great ambition and energy, MacNab went far in the world. As a young man he distinguished himself in the War of 1812 and emerged as one of its heroes. Later he fought the rebels in the Mackenzie Rebellion in 1837 and won the appreciation of the British Government, and eventually a knighthood. He became one of Hamilton's first lawyers and was a land speculator who amassed a great deal of wealth.

This attractive structure is probably what was called a "folly"; a structure that had no particular function but was built to grace the large rural estates of the English aristocracy. That is, it is most likely a bit of architectural fluff. MacNab modelled his life and property after this class.

He was elected to the provincial legislature and during a thirty-year political career became Prime Minister of Upper Canada. He was part of the inner circle, and had a great deal of skill and influence which he used to further his business ends. The castle reflected his social ambition to be part of the upper classes—a position he readily achieved. It was completed in 1838, just before Victoria ascended the throne, and was built in the Regency Style with an Italian influence. It overlooks his greatest achievement: the rail yards that lay below, beside the Bay.

He was the driving force in bringing the railroad to Hamilton. As director and chief promoter of a number of railway companies he helped to establish a network of steel tracks that strengthened Hamilton's position as a market centre. The wilderness to the west of Hamilton was rapidly being replaced by farms producing wheat and timber. These were products that needed an outlet to world markets, and Hamilton's location at the head of navigation on Lake Ontario was a natural transhipment point. He used his influence not only provincially, to incorporate the railway companies, but he mingled with royalty and

the moneyed upper classes in England to raise the needed capital. This latter capability was of great importance, since at this time British financing of railway building was indispensable.

MacNab, terminally burned out, died at the age of 64 in 1862. While it was quickly recognised that his property would make a fine city park, it was the end of the century before the city fathers in their collective wisdom got around to buying it. It then became an "unorthodox museum" full of local collectibles, and an aviary was created on the grounds. As part of Hamilton's centennial project in 1967, the castle was structurally rehabilitated and architecturally restored to its full Regency glory. It is now a classic period piece.

Rear View of the Castle

Under the orange beams of this lift bridge pass huge lake freighters carrying iron ore and coal. With the expansion of the Welland Canal, a task that was completed in 1887, it became possible to import cheaply by water both iron ore from the great reserves of the Lake Superior region and coal from the Appalachian fields. What the rivers of Appalachia had done for the industries of Pittsburgh, the Great Lakes and their canals would now do for Hamilton—allow for the economical assembly of massive amounts of raw material to be transformed into iron and steel and sold to nearby markets. The first pig iron was smelted in 1895 and the first steel was produced in 1900. Before this time, all the iron and steel that was used in manufacturing had to be imported.

From the banks of the Desjardins Canal, three bridges can be seen—two railway structures in the background, and nearest, the High Level Bridge. The twin concrete bridges that carry Highway 403 are farther to the left of the picture.

Also farther left is a new structure that, while not very photogenic, has important ecological implications. The narrow passage separating Cootes Paradise from the Bay is now straddled by a steel "Fishway." Its purpose is to control the passage of fish between the two bodies of water—more specifically, to keep carp out of the marsh. Carp have been the principle agents responsible for the destruction of marsh vegetation such as cattails, and have greatly reduced the value of the marsh as wildlife habitat. Originally, a series of dikes were to have been built that would have kept carp out of large areas of the marsh—but this proposal was rejected by the federal Department of Fisheries, on the grounds that insufficient attention had been paid to fish spawning grounds. The fish population migrates into the marsh from the Bay during the spring, and out in the fall. The Fishway allows all small fish to enter, but the larger ones are trapped and hand sorted. Desirable species such as pickerel and pike are allowed in, while carp are sent back to the Bay.

This was the typical appearance of the wooden sheds that were found around the bay 100 years ago.

Ice fishing was a common activity until the 1920's, by which time increased pollution took its toll. The shacks around the Desjardins Canal were gradually removed when the area was relandscaped during the beautification activities of the 1930's.

Small steam vessels such as the *Modjeska*, pictured here, were common before the age of the automobile and provided the population with an inexpensive means of travel to the Bay's north shore and amusement parks, or just for holiday excursions.

The appearance of the 19th century harbour was decidedly different from the harbour of today. Graceful schooners sailed the Great Lakes, and simple but aesthetically appealing wooden sheds served as harbour buildings. The water was clean enough and the winters still sufficiently cold to allow ice fishing—a practice that died out in the late 1920's due to pollution. The cutting of ice for summer refrigeration was also part of the seasonal cycle. In the warmer weather, excursion steamers criss-crossed the bay with holidaying townsfolk.

James Street access at the turn of the last century. The southwest corner of Hamilton has always been a prestige location: one where large homes on spacious estates were built upon the raised foot of the Escarpment. The land here was dry, often with a view to the Bay, and close to the core of the city. Gradually the large estates upon which many of the early homes were built grew very valuable and were severed off and subdivided. Large and prestigious houses were put on tiny lots without much elbow room. Today few even moderate-sized properties remain.

This picture of a property called Ballinahinch was taken about 1890. Note the tent, which may have been used to serve refreshments for the endless social gatherings that were and are typical of the socially prominent. As has happened with almost all of the large estates, the property seen here was severed off. This structure is still alive and well and has become a condominium. It is near James Street South just where the road begins its ascent of the Escarpment. It was designed by William Thomas, the same architect who created St. Paul's Presbyterian Church (see page 7).

Waterdown was a mill town founded in the early 1800's where Grindstone Creek descends the Escarpment. Lumber and grist mills were among the first to appear when the land was being cleared for agriculture and the soil put into agricultural production. With the advent of steam power, and the reduction of a dependable supply of water that followed the loss of tree cover, the mills became uneconomical and over a period of time as they burned down they were not rebuilt. The town stagnated economically for many years until in the latter part of this century it became a bedroom community for Hamilton and Toronto.

The stone buildings constructed to house the activities of the time are a legacy of the early period of Waterdown's history. This two-storey commercial block (right) which wraps around the corner of Mill and Dundas Streets in the core of the early town, was one of the earliest structures and was likely built in the 1820's. It and the structure above were built of uncoursed limestone quarried locally. Both structures have housed a wide variety of activities such as a harness shop, bakery, feed mill, jam factory, bank, artisans' shops and the present bookstore.

Battlefield House

In Battlefield Park, this inscription is found at the base of the 125-foot-high monument commemorating a decisive battle that took place in 1813 :

"In the dead of night the British advanced from Burlington Heights and surprising the enemy, put him to confusion. This is held to have been the decisive engagement in the War of 1812-13. Here the tide of invasion was met and turned by the pioneer patriots and soldiers of the King of one hundred years ago."

An American force had crossed the Niagara River and was advancing along the shore of Lake Ontario. Their encampment at the Gage farm was noticed by a boy named Billy Green (Hamilton's own Paul Revere), who informed the commander of the badly outnumbered British forces. With about 700 men he attacked by night an encampment of over 3,000 American soldiers, which eventually led to the American force withdrawing back across the border.

At the turn of the 19th century it was decided to commemorate this War of 1812 victory with a monument. The local historical society, dominated by the local upper crust, was split between men and women on how to proceed. The women formed their own historical group, took over, and did things their way. The men had sought a different site, closer to where the actual fighting had taken place.

Battlefield House, as the frame house came to be called, was built around 1796 as a 1½- storey house and expanded to a full two stories in 1830. It was restored at the turn of the century and made into a museum, which it still is today.

This mill in Albion Mills was built by United Empire Loyalists at the end of the 18ᵗʰ century and was part of a small community typical of the time, having the usual mills, a general store, blacksmith shops, and

Albion Falls

a number of hotels. The name Mud Street, which is still in use today, reflected the state of the roads at the time. This mill remained in use until 1907 when one of its owners was accidentally killed in it. Portions of the stone foundation and the wheel-pit can still be seen today. Albion, by the way, is another name for Britain.

Houses on Victoria Street

The houses on these two pages typify the rich heritage of domestic architecture found in Dundas. Like Hamilton, Dundas strove to become a commercial and trading centre. Like Hamilton, it became instead an industrial community with foundries, machine-building factories, cotton and woollen mills, to name a few. The wealth generated by this industrial base in the last half of the nineteenth century was used in part to build numerous tasteful and well-designed homes. Neighbourhoods of this kind are found just north of King Street, a part of town also favoured for the construction of churches. The factories that helped give life to these houses in Dundas are now all but gone. However, supported by wealth from a broader area, the community has preserved both the homes and neighbourhoods.

This picturesque plant, located on Burlington Street, is used to make carbon black which is used by other industries as a raw material. The tire industry, for example, uses it in the rubber manufacturing process.

Adjacent to the Chedoke Civic Golf Course, steep slopes of the Escarpment are used during the winter as a ski run with a vertical drop of about 330 feet. Snow is built up to a great depth to create a safe run, and can take some time to melt away.

Webster's Falls, where Spencer Creek flows into the Spencer Gorge, is one of the jewels of the Niagara Escarpment.